STITCHING THE INTIFADA

Embroidery and Resistance in Palestine

Rachel Dedman

Common Threads Press

PREFACE

Stitching the Intifada

I write this at a time of genocide in Gaza, when relentless horrors are unfolding in front of our eyes. Amid incredible human loss and collective trauma, speaking about clothing may seem unimportant, even trivial. However, as I hope this essay will make clear, tatreez — the rich Palestinian tradition of embroidery — constitutes more than heritage. Tatreez is Palestinian life. In its repetitive binding of thread to fabric, embroidery involves the very simplest of gestures, and is a practice that embodies resilience.

One catalyst for this publication is the exhibition *Material Power: Palestinian Embroidery*,[1] which I curated for Kettle's Yard and The Whitworth in the UK. The exhibition explores over a century of Palestinian embroidery, dress and material culture, celebrating the rich traditions of tatreez and examining the ways it has transformed over time into an instrument of resistance and an ubiquitous commodity. *Material Power* brings together garments, archival material and commissioned film, as well as the work of contemporary artists, to reflect upon embroidery's continued capacity as a creative medium today.

Material Power grew out of a decade of work that I have done on the subject of Palestinian embroidery. In 2014, the Palestinian Museum in Birzeit, the West Bank, commissioned me to curate an exhibition on tatreez in Beirut, Lebanon, where I was living and working as an independent curator. Part of the reason I was commissioned for this was my privilege of mobility, of passports allowing me to travel in both Lebanon and Palestine for research, a freedom denied to nationals of either place. The first exhibition I curated, *At the Seams: A Political History of Palestinian Embroidery*, at Dar El-Nimer for Arts and Culture in 2016, birthed an expanded edition, entitled *Labour of Love: New Approaches to Palestinian Embroidery*, at the Palestinian Museum's main

---

[1] *Material Power: Palestinian Embroidery* was an exhibition curated by Rachel Dedman for Kettle's Yard, Cambridge (8 July – 29 October 2023), and The Whitworth, Manchester (24 November 2023 – 7 April 2024).

site in 2018. In between, I co-curated an exhibition at Beirut Art Centre with Marie Muracciole titled *Unravelled*, bringing together contemporary artists from all over the world who utilise embroidery and textile in their work.

From the very beginning of my research, much of the work of learning about tatreez came from meeting extraordinary people, spending time with embroiderers, curators and collectors such as Widad Kawar and Malak Al-Husseini Abdulrahim, Maha Abu Shosheh, Baha Jubeh, and George Al-Ama. Wherever I went, amazing people would throw open their attics, their wardrobes, their chests full of *thobes* (embroidered dresses), pulling them out one by one and telling me their stories. They taught me to 'read' Palestinian embroidery, to identify garments by their places of origin, to understand the craft intimately. Despite embroidered clothing being an indisputably physical thing, so much of tatreez lives in oral tradition — as knowledge passed down in person, over coffee.

While I immersed myself in the history of the craft, it also felt imperative to approach and understand tatreez as something alive and active, not confined to the past. I set about meeting women who continue to embroider today in Palestine, Lebanon and Jordan. I commissioned Maeve Brennan, an artist who was also living in Beirut at the time, to film these interviews. The film that Maeve made, entitled *The Embroiderers*, and the shorter videos she created from the many beautiful encounters we had, have featured in every exhibition I have made on this subject [Fig. 1]. They brought Palestinian women's voices into the heart of the exhibition, offering their contemporary perspectives on historical material.

Notions of resistance loomed large from the start. Embroidery has, perhaps, an unlikely role in the charged context of protest. And yet, in both loud and quiet ways, in public and private, the history of the craft is bound up in Palestinian struggles for freedom and nationhood. Embroidery, in symbolic as much as in physical form, has played a fundamental part in the articulation of

Figure 1: Still from Maeve Brennan's film, *The Embroiderers*, 2016, 23'04. Courtesy of the artist.

Palestinian nationalism after 1948, and resistance remains a lens through which to understand the practice in its current form. As Subhiye Krayem, an embroiderer we met in Ein el-Hilweh camp in Lebanon, puts it: 'Folklore is a politics unto itself. It means that I exist.'

This publication focuses on the relationship between embroidery and resistance in Palestine, told through the core objects and ideas of *Material Power*, and the research that underpins them. My work seeks to understand and frame Palestinian embroidery as a continually evolving practice, from the late nineteenth century through to the present day. Made by people and worn on the body, clothing is embedded in the political, social and economic dynamics of its time, and in the emotional life of its maker. For me, embroidery offers us an intimate vehicle for unfolding a human history of place. ⬥

WHAT IS PALESTINIAN EMBROIDERY?

Tatreez is Palestine's pre-eminent cultural practice, its most famous product. Palestinian embroidered dress is best known in its most spectacular form — through the festive wedding and occasion dresses women would spend years embroidering from their girlhood onwards.[2] *Material Power*, however, opens not with these extraordinary celebration garments, but with clothing that is not usually written about, or collected, or presented in exhibition: the humbler dresses that women wore every day in the late nineteenth and early twentieth centuries. For me, these everyday dresses capture how we might think about all Palestinian embroidery, as material evidence of rural women's lives, and as inherently mutable things.

On an everyday dress from Widad Kawar's collection [Fig. 2], the traces of its maker's labour are visible in her garment. Two openings on either side of the chest panel indicate how she would have breastfed her baby; these have been sewn closed once the child was weaned. The patches on her elbows and at her knees suggest how she might have knelt to work clay, wash vegetables or clean clothes. In my mind's eye I imagine her wiping wet hands on soft linen day in and day out, until the surface wears away to threads and needs to be replaced. This image of that same dress turned inside-out [Fig. 3] gives a full sense of the mosaic, palimpsestic nature of its construction and evolution over time.

---

2 Shelagh Weir, *Embroidery from Palestine* (University of Washington Press, 2006), 9. For further reading on the history of tatreez and Palestinian material culture, see: Widad Kawar, *Threads of Identity* (Rimal Books, 2011); Jehan Rejab, *Palestinian Costume* (Kegan Paul International, 1989); Shelagh Weir, *Palestinian Costume* (British Museum Press, 1989); Rachel Dedman, *At the Seams: A Political History of Palestinian Embroidery* (The Palestinian Museum, 2016); Rachel Dedman and Shuruq Harb, eds., *Labour of Love: New Approaches to Palestinian Embroidery* (The Palestinian Museum, 2018); Wafa Ghnaim, *Tatreez and Tea: Embroidery and Storytelling in the Palestinian Diaspora* (2018).

Figures 2 [above] and 3 [opposite]: Everyday dress from 'Ajjur village, near Hebron, 1900s–1920s, from the collection of Tiraz: Widad Kawar Home for Arab Dress. Image by Tanya Traboulsi, courtesy of the Palestinian Museum.

Stitching the Intifada

On another everyday dress [Fig. 4], the once bright red thread on the side panels has been bleached by long exposure to the sun. The back reveals the 'handwriting' of the embroidery varies too: one section is stitched more boldly than the other, and on a darker base of linen. Perhaps the owner of this dress inherited a garment from her mother or grandmother, discarded the worn bits, and incorporated its embroidery onto her existing base.

I find such humble garments extremely compelling. Such clothing resists notions of the definitive museum object, with a singular maker and clear date of production. Rather, these everyday dresses transform materially over time, passing into other hands. I love the idea that a dress starts life in one form, and over the years has bits added to it or replaced so often that by the end of its life not one patch of the original remains, and yet it is still the same dress. These garments are a reminder to understand tatreez as mutable and adaptive, changing alongside the woman who wears it. ◈

Figure 4 [opposite]: Everyday dress from Hebron, 1930–1935, from the collection of Tiraz: Widad Kawar Home for Arab Dress. Image by Tanya Traboulsi, courtesy of the Palestinian Museum.

Figure 5 [overleaf]: Forest of dresses in *Material Power: Palestinian Embroidery* at Kettle's Yard, Cambridge. Photo: Jo Underhill.

EMBROIDERY AS LANGUAGE

Tatreez is often described as a rich visual language, one shared by women. In Palestine in the late nineteenth century, the way a woman dressed and the decisions she made around her embroidery spoke to her character, her identity, her origins.[3] Indeed, partly what makes Palestinian dress remarkable is its regional variety, with each area — even individual villages — defined by recognisable colours, cuts, motifs, stitches and textiles.[4]

Dress changed over the course of a woman's lifetime: from childhood (girls learned to embroider at a young age, and spent years creating a trousseau of garments to take into marriage), to later life, when dress and embroidery became simpler and more austere to reflect maturity. The wedding was the most important rite of passage of a woman's life, and her embroidered wedding dress perhaps the most special thing she owned.[5] The 'forest' of dresses in *Material Power* [Fig. 4] brought together such celebratory garments from all over Palestine.

The area around Hebron is associated with a motif called the *khayam el-basha*, or 'Pasha's tent', seen here on a *ghudfeh*, or head covering [Fig. 6]. Dense cross-stitch embroidery of this kind, in pinks and reds, is the most typical Palestinian style, and inspiration for motifs was drawn from local flora, food, architecture, and daily life.[6] Figure 7 is a *jellayeh* from the Hebron area (with influences from nearby Beit Dajan), recognisable from the silk patchwork up the front of the skirt. Typically, the front of these dresses were split up to the waist, so the skirt would have flapped open as a woman walked, with a garment underneath. However, in the British Mandate period from 1918, conventions of modesty became more conservative, with the result that women sewed these up or buttoned them closed. In an image of the garment inside-out [Fig. 8], there are buttons visible along the inside. The *jellayeh*

---

3   Kawar, *Threads of Identity*, 63.

4   Rajab, *Palestinian Costume*, 10.

5   Weir, *Palestinian Costume*, 74.

6   Margarita Skinner, *Palestinian Embroidery Motifs: A Treasury of Stitches, 1850–1950* (Rimal Books, 2007), 37, 111.

Figure 6: *Ghudfeh* from Hebron, 1920–1930,
from the collection of Malak Al-Husseini Abdulrahim.
Image by Tanya Traboulsi, courtesy of the Palestinian Museum.

Figures 7 and 8: *Jellayeh* from Hebron/Beit Dajan, 1900–1915,
from the collection of The Palestinian Heritage Museum, Dar Al-Tifel Al-Arabi.
Images by Kayané Antreassian, courtesy of the Palestinian Museum.

speaks to the ways in which clothing reflected the shifting socio-political dynamics of its day.

Women from Bethlehem, meanwhile, were famous for couching, or *tahriri*, an embroidery technique that involves laying thick cord on top of a garment in twisted patterns — often with gold or silver thread. This *taqsireh* jacket [Fig. 9] would have been worn over a velvet dress, or a cotton one with long pointed sleeves. Bethlehem was a popular pilgrimage town, whose visitors boosted the local economy, and many Bethlehemite men in the late nineteenth and early twentieth centuries emigrated to South America for work and sent back remittances.[7] This greater local prosperity was reflected in the richness of embellishment on women's clothing. Brides based elsewhere might also commission couched elements from Bethlehem as a mark of status. For example, a Ramallah dress with Bethlehem sleeves [Fig. 10] indicates the presence of a cottage industry for certain types of Palestinian embroidery in the early twentieth century.[8]

---

7   Kawar, *Threads of Identity*, 139.

8   Ibid., 142.

Figure 9: *Taqsireh* jacket from Bethlehem, with British cotton lining, c. 1900, from the collection of George M. Al-Ama. Image by Kayané Antreassian, courtesy of the Palestinian Museum.

Figure 10: Al-Bireh dress with Bethlehem couched sleeves, 1930s–1940s, from the collection of Birzeit University Museum. Image by Kayané Antreassian, courtesy of the Palestinian Museum.

The use of imported British cotton on the yoke of a dress, or for the lining of jackets, was also a subtle status symbol — a sign a woman could afford pieces of foreign fabric. Machine-made embroidery served a similar purpose at a time when access to sewing machines was a luxury. When DMC (Dollfus-Mieg & Cie, a French thread company) entered the Palestinian market in the 1930s, thread was sold with waste canvas, which enabled women to embroider on a wider range of textiles, and with pattern books, which offered women inspiration from abroad.[9] Motifs like 'foreign moon' or 'foreign rainbow' entered the embroiderer's lexicon at this time.

In the Galilee, embroidery tended to be less dense, with a different style to the patterning of the stitchwork. Women tended to wear coats accompanied by shirts or *shirwal* pants. The story goes that embroidery was lighter-touch in this region because of how hard women worked in the fields. Galilee was an agricultural centre for Palestine in the nineteenth century and during the civil war in the United States in the 1860s, when North American cotton production slowed down, the crop was grown in greater volume in the Mediterranean.[10] As a result, Galilean women spent more time in the fields and less time embroidering, associating the practice with the waste of money and spare time enjoyed by Southern Palestinians.[11] Women did still embroider, of course, with a wealth of stitches different to those popular in central Palestine, but local dress also relied on a richer variety of fabrics from Aleppo and Damascus, such as beautiful ikat silk, thanks to the Galilee's proximity to Syria.[12]

---

[9] Weir, *Palestinian Costume*, 42–43.

[10] Alexander Scholch, 'European penetration and the economic development of Palestine, 1856–82', in *Studies in the Economic and Social History of Palestine in the Nineteenth and Twentieth Centuries*, ed. Roger Owen (Southern Illinois University Press, 1982), 14.

[11] Weir, *Embroidery from Palestine*, 14.

[12] See Tania Tamari Nasir, Omar Joseph Nasser-Khoury, Shirabe Yamada, with Widad Kamel Kawar, *Seventeen Embroidery Techniques from Palestine: An Instruction Manual* (Sunbula, 2019).

Figure 11: Dress from Gaza, 1940s, from the collection of Dar Al-Tifel Al-Arabi Museum for Palestinian Heritage. Image by Kayané Antreassian, courtesy of the Palestinian Museum.

Gaza is an area known for its use of vibrant pinks and a sparser, geometric approach to embroidery. A v-shaped neckline was typical [Fig. 11], along with a motif known as the *qeladeh* or necklace, which meant the embroidery acted as a type of permanent jewellery. Such jewellery traditionally served a talismanic function, and there is something beautiful, poetic and tragic about the ancestors of Gazan women carrying on their body a permanent protective power.

These are just a few examples of Palestinian embroidery's richness and diversity. *Material Power* goes into detail about each geographic region, as well as the role of colour, the range of textiles, and the meaning of motifs, immersing a visitor in the complexities of the practice and equipping them with the ability to 'read' and understand the dresses they are seeing.

Historically, embroidery was very much a rural woman's craft, as middle and upper class Palestinians had long adopted Ottoman and European dress by the mid-nineteenth century. However, one unusual garment in the exhibition [Fig. 12] complicates that distinction. It's a buttery-soft silk slip dress, sleeveless, cut in European style, with a little jacket over the top, embroidered with Palestinian motifs. It was bought by a woman called Basma Kawar in 1921, while on her honeymoon. It's interesting because it indicates the presence of an early cottage industry in Palestine catering to the well-to-do and offering tasteful traditional touches to modern fashion for those who would otherwise have little to do with rural communities and their dress.

Figure 12: Silk dress, 1921, from the collection of Tiraz: Widad Kawar Home for Arab Dress. Photo: Jo Underhill, courtesy of Kettle's Yard, Cambridge.

Meanwhile, Figure 13 looks at first glance like a Palestinian rural family captured in their typical, traditional garb. In reality, this is an upper-class Palestinian family, who have visited a Jerusalem photo studio and dressed up in *fellahi* costume.[13] It is a reminder that a *thobe*, or embroidered dress, was for one Palestinian woman the most precious thing she owned, something she'd spent years making, and perhaps the only thing she took with her into exile. But for another Palestinian woman, of a different socio-economic background, a *thobe* was just something to put on as costume in auto-Orientalising play. These objects remind us how nuanced relationships to clothing can be, and of the multiple ways in which class and embroidery intersect in this period in Palestine. ◆

---

[13] See Karène Sanchez Summerer and Sary Zananiri, eds., *Imaging and Imagining Palestine: Photography, Modernity and the Biblical Lens, 1918–1948* (Brill, 2021).

Figure 13: Visitors in Jerusalem dressed in traditional clothing.
Photographed by Khalil Raad, 1910. Jerusalem, Palestine.
Gelatin silver developing-out paper print. 14.4 x 10 cm.
Fouad el Khoury Collection, courtesy of the Arab Image Foundation, Beirut.

THE EMBROIDERED WOMAN

The events of 1948, which Palestinians call the Nakba, or catastrophe, changed the lives of everyone in Palestine. Hundreds of thousands of Palestinians were forcibly displaced from their homes by Zionist forces, and many were killed or injured in the battle to keep their land from dispossession.[14] It feels difficult to do justice to the full horror and impact of the Nakba in such facts and statistics, which can feel too cold and impersonal. The dress in Figure 14, however, embodies the intimate realities of the Nakba and its effect on people.

The cut, colour and motifs of this dress tell us that it was originally made by a woman from Ramallah. In 1948, she donated it to another woman, who had been displaced from her home during the Nakba and walked into the West Bank carrying with her little to wear except what she had on. We can see, however, that the woman who inherited the dress must have been bigger than the original embroiderer, as the garment has been enlarged via a series of panels at the sides and around the waist. The material used for the enlargement is sacking from a bag of flour issued by UNRWA (the United Nations Refugee Works Agency), of the kind given out to refugees after the crisis. You can just make out the *nuun* (the letter 'n') from the word *tahin*, flour, stamped on the side in UN blue. The very materiality of the dress, therefore, speaks not only to the urgency of the situation, but also to the generosity and resilience of women at what must have been one of the most difficult moments of their lives.

In *Material Power*, I've placed the 'Nakba dress' close to a contemporary work by the artist Aya Haidar. Haidar's *Safe Space* series [Fig. 15] documents her mother's memories of growing up during the Civil War in Lebanon and the simple everyday actions her family took to stay safe. From a distance the round

---

14   For further information about the events of the Nakba, see the websites of the United Nations https://www.un.org/unispal/about-the-nakba/ and Amnesty International https://nakba.amnesty.org/en/about/, both accessed 8 June 2024; and Kristian Coates Urichsen, *A Dictionary of Politics in the Middle East* (Oxford University Press, 2018).

Figure 14 [above]: Dress from Ramallah, 1930s, from the collection of Maha Abu Shosheh. Image by Kayané Antreassian, courtesy of the Palestinian Museum.

Figure 15 [opposite]: Aya Haidar, *Safe Space* series, 2023.
Photo: Jo Underhill, courtesy of Kettle's Yard, Cambridge.

Stitching the Intifada

embroidered samplers seem bright and playful, but as one comes closer, the stories are dark. The family would wear pots and pans on their head to protect from stray bullets flying in through the windows, and pan lids on their torso to the market, in case of snipers. They slept under their beds for months in case the roof caved in during an air raid. Aya's grandmother got so fed up at having to constantly pick glass from their shattered windows out of the furniture that they piled it all up in the middle of the room, and sat on the carpet. While these simple stitched scenes are ostensibly about a different conflict (although geo-politically they are very much entwined), for me they capture, just like the Nakba dress, the human experience of conflict. They speak to the ability of embroidery and textiles to bear witness, hold memory and tell stories, and in so doing constitute a quiet form of resistance in themselves.

Embroidery, of course, did not die after the Nakba — it persisted and it transformed. Many women were living in dire circumstances, either abroad as refugees, or at home under occupation, in either case divorced from their former lives in agriculture and the local economic and social networks that enabled embroidery as a practice.[15] The New Dress, or Camp Dress, emerged in response to these changes. The regional variation of embroidery slowly eroded as women from different areas of Palestine lived together in camps, and the forms of the dress homogenised — particularly into the *shawal* or 'six branch' styles seen in Figure 16. What I find fascinating about these dresses is that while they may not have quite the same richness of material or refinement of approach as the historical examples I've cited, they still tell us something compelling about the women who made them. It takes a bold woman to wear a lime green dress with day-glo orange embroidery. And although it is made of inexpensive polyester likely imported from China, with motifs inspired by the magazines its maker was reading in the 1980s or '90s, the garment speaks to women's ability to renew and evolve the craft.

---

15   Kawar, *Threads of Identity*, 415.

At the same time, in the decades following 1948 there was a concerted revival of traditional Palestinian heritage, prompted in part by the appropriation and erasure of Palestinian culture by the Israeli occupation. In this process of revival, the rural *fellahi* woman became symbolic of what I call the 'Palestinian pastoral'. She was evidence of the historic presence of Palestinians on their land, as eternal as the natural world to which she is connected, and always identified by her embroidered dress. The 'embroidered woman', as I call her, became a pre-eminent symbol in the decades to follow. She was popularised by Palestinian Liberation Artists, who in the 1970s took her up as a key figure in painting and ceramics, such as in a beautiful work by Vera Tamari [Fig. 17]. Many artists continue to do so today.

The Village Awakens, 1987, by Sliman Mansour [Fig. 18], is one of the most iconic paintings of modern Palestine. Here the embroidered woman's body is blown up to the scale of the landscape, the curves of her head and shoulders continuous with the rolling hills and rooftops beside her. And then, in a not terribly subtle metaphor, from between her legs a torrent of men bursts forth, ready to toil the land and create culture. The embroidered woman is the embodiment of generative fertility, she is literally the motherland. On the one hand, such images signalled an important shift in value: for the first time, women who had little cultural or political visibility in Palestine featured large-scale on paintings. On the other hand, such images had the effect of reducing the embroidered woman to a simplified signifier. ◈

Figure 16 [overleaf]: New Dresses as displayed in *Material Power: Palestinian Embroidery* at the Whitworth, University of Manchester (2023).
Photo: Michael Pollard.

Stitching the Intifada

Figure 17: Vera Tamari, *Palestinian Women at Work*, 1979.
Ceramic relief, collection of Dr. Ibrahim Khalil Lada'a.
Image by Kayané Antreassian, courtesy of the Palestinian Museum.

Stitching the Intifada

Figure 18 [above]: Sliman Mansour, *The Village Awakens*, 1987. Courtesy of the artist.

Figure 19 [overleaf]: Selection of posters from *Material Power: Palestinian Embroidery* at Kettle's Yard, Cambridge. Photo: Jo Underhill.

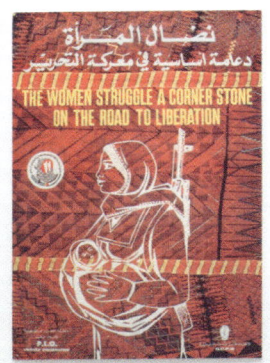

8

THE PALESTINIAN
FOLKLORE
WORLD DAY

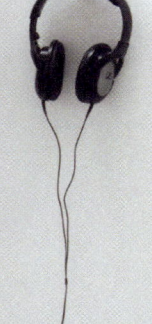

11

9

EMBROIDERY AND THE INTIFADA

Images of the 'embroidered woman' began to circulate as posters from the 1970s onwards, both in Palestine and abroad [Fig. 19]. In them, embroidery often appeared alongside other symbols of the nation, such as oranges from Jaffa and the city of Jerusalem. In the three posters of Figure 20, the embroidered woman's body becomes a literal extension of the land itself. In each one, her hair is the flag of the nation, the wheat she harvests, or the very body of other farmers and fighters.

In the same period, the Palestinian Liberation Organisation (PLO) pioneered the travel of Palestinian exhibitions all over the world. They took shows of embroidered dress and other Palestinian crafts to East Germany, Moscow and Japan. Tamam Al Akhal, an artist who ran the Arts and Heritage section of the PLO with Ismail Shammout, described how the exhibitions of embroidery they organised were backdrops to high-profile political meetings, such as Yasser Arafat meeting the king of Spain. Such exhibitions meant embroidery served as a form of 'soft diplomacy'; this shifted tatreez into an international realm, out of its original context. Divorced from the body, it was instrumentalised in public displays of nationhood.

Back in Palestine, posters began to evolve: the embroidered women retained the strength and tenderness of motherhood, but took on armed iconography as the Palestinian resistance movement gathered momentum. In 1987, the First Intifada begun — a national-scale, popular uprising by the Palestinian people against the Israeli military occupation of the West Bank and Gaza. As young men were increasingly arrested or shot at protests, women took on a visible role in frontline struggle. In this period it was illegal to show Palestinian colours in public or to fly the Palestinian flag, so women started to embroider explicit symbols of resistance onto garments — creating 'Intifada dresses' [Fig. 21].[16]

Visible on Intifada dresses are traditional motifs embroidered in Palestinian national colours, mingling amongst a new symbolic vocabulary. On one dress, a dove soars across a chest panel flanked by rifles and love hearts. Important Palestinian architectural sites like the Dome of the Rock or Al-Aqsa mosque became popular new motifs, alongside the map of Palestine and its flag. Many include text, such as the word 'Palestine' in English and Arabic, or signs of connection to political parties, like the letters 'PLO'. On several, at the lower panel on the back of the dress, women stitched a ship of return sailing home to Palestine.[17]

Such dresses are indisputably powerful garments, which render women's bodies sites of explicit political resistance. What is also extraordinary about them is that they feel at odds with the typical material culture of protest. When most of us attend a demonstration, we make things that are quick or spontaneous: scrawled signs and printed posters. But as anyone who has ever embroidered will know, these dresses are the very opposite of fast. Embroidery is an incredibly slow form of labour, and Intifada dresses are the result of months, if not years of work. They were in many cases stitched in secret, perhaps without electricity, while a village was under siege. In their visual form, as well as in the conditions of their making, such garments embody the notion of *sumud* — steadfastness — that is central to the Intifada itself. The extended temporality of embroidery reflects the idea that resistance in Palestine is a process, not an event.

---

16 The military order criminalising Palestinians attending and organising protests of any kind, and displaying the Palestinian flag, has been in place since 1967. The order was lifted after the signing of the Oslo Accords but quickly reintroduced by Israel, and continues to apply in the West Bank today. Other laws, including one passed in 2023, prohibit the use of the Palestinian flag anywhere in occupied territory. For more information see Amnesty International's press release, 'Israel/OPT: new restrictions on Palestinian flags an attempt to 'legitimise racism'', 11 January 2023, accessed online 4 June 2024.

17 See Kawar, *Threads of Identity*, 429–431.

Figure 20a: Abdel Rahman Al-Muzayen, 'Glory to the Revolution', published by FATAH, 1979. Courtesy of the Palestine Poster Project Archives.

Figure 20b: Mohammed Roukwie, 'International Women's Day',
published by Palestine Women's Association, c.1990.
Courtesy of the Palestine Poster Project Archives.

Figure 20c: Abdel Rahman Al-Muzayen, '29th November',
published by the League of Arab States, 1984.
Courtesy of the Palestine Poster Project Archives.

Figures 21 [above] and 22 [overleaf]: Intifada dresses, 1987–1993, from the collection of Tiraz: Widad Kawar Home for Arab Dress. Photo: Jo Underhill, courtesy of Kettle's Yard, Cambridge.

Another context in which embroidery constitutes a form of resistance — to the Israeli occupation and to challenging circumstances — is among men who practice embroidery while being held as political prisoners in Israeli prisons. In Palestine the vast majority of embroiderers are female, and the craft is the preserve of women. Some of the women I met in the course of my research, for whom embroidery is their livelihood, told me that their husbands or sons might help them with stitchwork, but that this isn't something most men would admit to doing publicly. However, in the indisputably masculine context of the prison, embroidery is something men speak about with pride.

The lampshade pieces in Figure 23 represent a creative collaboration between Nawal, from Walaja, and her son Hatim, who is imprisoned by Israel. The two would exchange the lampshades back and forth, building and embroidering them together in a collaborative process. Such pieces reflect a time when craft materials were allowed into prison by the Israeli authorities. In these periods, the work prisoners make is more elaborate. At times when it is banned, craft objects are more improvised. Prisoners speak of hoarding olive stones for beading, using cereal box cardboard as the basis for stitchwork, of smuggling needles in the spines of books and pulling threads from their towels.

What I love about such objects is that while the use of Palestinian colours reflects their maker's national pride, these are pieces also characterised by tenderness: things made for wives and daughters, for Mother's Day and International Women's Day. In Figure 24 is work by my Palestinian Museum colleague Karam Al-Maloukh who made gifts for his wife, Alaa, including a bag out of reinforced cardboard and velvet, which carries their initials on either side. The bag is decorated with the same 'prisoner's stitch' found on Nawal and Hatim's lampshades.

The resilience of such gestures and the softness of their content defy simplistic notions of embroidery as 'women's work' and challenge its incompatibility with the masculine. Although both resistance and embroidery tend to be gendered activities, such objects trouble the distinctions and the definitions of both, and suggest that while embroidery has — as we have seen in paintings and posters — contributed to the construction of gendered roles, it can also mediate in their refusal.

Figure 23: Hatim Al Araj, embroidered decorative pieces, 2005.
Embroidery, beads, sequins, made in Ofer prison.
Image by Kayané Antreassian, courtesy of the Palestinian Museum.

Figure 24: Karam Al-Maloukh, embroidered bag, 2008.
Silk, textile, and cardboard, made in Al-Naqab prison.
Image by Kayané Antreassian, courtesy of the Palestinian Museum.

Contemporary artwork is incorporated throughout *Material Power*, speaking to the historical material it sits among. The work of Palestinian artist Khalil Rabah appears alongside the Intifada dresses and prison-made objects. In *Tattoo*, 1996 [Fig. 26], Rabah has removed the black thread from the central panel of a keffiyeh, a textile we all recognise and associate with Palestinian resistance. Yet despite the threads' removal, the outline of the pattern remains visible still, albeit ghostly: the symbol, even if defiled, cannot be so straightforwardly undermined. The threads sit beneath the denuded keffiyeh like hair, reminding us of the body — vulnerable, intimate, but enduring — behind the symbol. ◆

Figure 25 [overleaf]: Karam Al-Maloukh, embroidered book, 2006.
Mixed media, made in Ofer prison.
Image by Kayané Antreassian, courtesy of the Palestinian Museum.

Figure 26 [opposite]: Khalil Rabah, *Tattoo*, 1996.
Photo: Jo Underhill, courtesy of Kettle's Yard, Cambridge.

FROM LOVE TO LABOUR

The last chapter of the exhibition tells a different story of embroidery after 1948. While tatreez was in the process of being politicised, it was also being commodified. Embroidery is rarely worn by women on a day-to-day basis today, and is instead most visible as product: cushion, keyring, bag or wallet. The ones in Figure 27 were mass-produced in China, but a great deal of Palestinian embroidered products today are handmade by women working for charities and NGOs.

The events of 1948 triggered the foundation of several important charitable organisations who used embroidery after the Nakba as a way of providing women an immediate income. In the years that followed, embroidery became a commodity, shifting from a labour of love — something made by a woman, for herself alone — to paid labour, as something that circulated in a global marketplace.

Figure 27: Ramallah, 2016. Courtesy of the author.

Figure 28: Photographs, 1969–1973, from the archive of Inaash Al-Mukhayim, courtesy of Inaash Association.

The images in Figure 28 come from the archive of Inaash al-Mukhayim, Beirut, and show the kinds of embroidered products the organisation was making in the 1970s, employing Palestinian women in Lebanon's refugee camps. Inaash Association, as they are known, catered to a middle and upper class Beiruti and diaspora market, and used embroidery in the fashioning of a modern Palestinian woman — one who wore green halterneck dresses and carried little embroidered handbags. These images are fascinating, but they are also evidence that by the 1970s it was the privileged few who could afford to own embroidery and to perform Palestinian identity and solidarity on their bodies and in their homes. The women who stitched those pieces, meanwhile, could not afford to keep what they made.

With the rise of the internet, the number of embroidery-producing NGOs has proliferated. My original research,

back in 2016, analysed over 100 such organisations, and scrutinised the rhetoric of 'female empowerment' that most claim to create.[18] Embroidery projects are easy for NGOs to start because they do not require much infrastructure, and women don't need to be educated. In the majority of cases embroiderers are paid by the piece, meaning the faster they stitch the quicker they earn. But if they are unable to work, because their child is sick or their parent needs care, a woman will not receive an income at the moment they need it most. Some cooperative models mitigate this income precarity, but risk remains because embroidery is a luxury good, without a constant market. The product is rightly expensive for the consumer, but embroiderers might receive just 10–25% of the price

---

18   See Dedman, *At the Seams: A Political History of Palestinian Embroidery*, which details the history of Palestinian embroidery NGOs and includes a database of 100 such organisations.

the customer pays, for what may have been weeks or months of work. In the majority of cases, embroiderers do not have any creative agency in the embroidery process, as design is managed by NGO organisers, and the gatekeeping of knowledge around embroidery's historical meaning is an attendant problem.

As a curator and art historian, for me it's vital to think critically about embroidery's production today because the financial and cultural value of the tatreez we buy is predicated upon these ambiguous notions of female 'empowerment'. Embroidery's purchase is implicitly posited as a form of resistance of its own, and explicitly as a gesture of solidarity with Palestine, while its making is embedded in a capitalist model underpinned by precarious labour and unequal access to knowledge, in a system that rarely makes any embroiderer financially independent or lifted beyond poverty.

However, it's also vital to acknowledge that for most of the women I interviewed, who embroider for organisations in villages and refugee camps across Palestine, Lebanon and Jordan, tatreez is a source of enormous pride. The opportunity to work and bring in an income, however modest, is absolutely essential, and can be transformative economically to an entire extended family. Beyond the financial, embroidery's connection to Palestinian identity is hugely significant, and many women — particularly those who are multiple-generation Palestinian refugees in Lebanon and Jordan — are inspired by the meaningful connection to their homeland that this work offers them. ◈

SOFT RESISTANCE: AN ENDING

I want to end by talking about two very different contemporary pieces. One is a new work by artist Mounira Al Solh, *Night Holes*, 2023 [Fig. 29]. In this installation, Al Solh uses the familiar, mass-produced textiles that are common as bed covers and blankets in family homes across the Levant. The artist has pierced their surface with small holes, and hemmed them with thread, a gesture that recalls her childhood memory of being frightened and unable to sleep during the Lebanese Civil War. At night her mother would allow her to rend small tears in her pyjamas and sew them shut as a form of meditative distraction.

Suspended in the gallery like tents, the hole-studded surface of the blankets might be read as bullet-pocked ceilings or skies full of stars. Accompanied by an audio installation of children singing lullabies and the sound of sewing and knitting, the work speaks to the experience of refugees, and the modest comfort found in needle and thread. *Night Holes* returns us to an idea at stake in *Material Power*, which is about how embroidery remains an articulate and meaningful medium for artists today, able to speak to the conditions of the present.

The final object in the exhibition is a dress [Fig. 30] by Raja El-Zeer, a professional embroiderer I met in Selfit, Palestine, in the course of my research. Raja made this dress for herself, to wear at her son's wedding in 2014. What I love about it is that it is not 'traditionally' Palestinian. From the all-over nature of the pattern, to the motif itself (when we met Raja showed us how she takes inspiration from Facebook and Pinterest and shares designs with her friends), to the tonal thread and colours and use of beads, a purist of Palestinian embroidery would not consider the *thobe* traditional, and by extension, may not consider it worthy of preservation or display or study.

Figure 29 [overleaf]: Mounira Al Solh, *Night Holes*, 2023.
Courtesy of the artist. Image from *Material Power: Palestinian Embroidery* at the Whitworth, University of Manchester (2023). Photo: Michael Pollard.

And yet, by virtue of being made by Raja, and worn by her, it is of course as much a Palestinian embroidered *thobe*, and vibrant example of tatreez, as any of the hundred-year-old garments I showed at the beginning.

These two very different recent pieces of embroidery prove that tatreez is a practice preserving itself, continuing to evolve and transform in line with the women who stitch it. In the ongoing struggle for freedom and the right of return, against occupation and genocide, embroidery remains a material manifestation of identity and hope in Palestine and beyond. In the hands of artists and embroiderers all over the world, tatreez constitutes a quiet resistance. ◈

Figure 30 [overleaf]: Image from *Material Power: Palestinian Embroidery* installation at the Whitworth, University of Manchester (2023).
Photo: Michael Pollard.

Figure 31 [opposite]: Intifada dresses, 1987–1993,
from the collection of Tiraz: Widad Kawar Home for Arab Dress.
Photo: Jo Underhill, courtesy of Kettle's Yard, Cambridge.

ACKNOWLEDGEMENTS

I've been privileged to work on and with tatreez for over a decade, and there are many people who have supported my research, my writing and the curation of exhibitions in Lebanon, Palestine and the UK. Heartfelt thanks to Widad Kawar and all the team at Tiraz, to Malak Al-Husseini Abdulrahim and Inaash Association, to Maha Abu Shosheh, George Al-Ama, and the team at Dar Al-Tifel Al-Arabi, to The Palestinian Museum, who first commissioned me to work on this in 2013, and my friend Baha Jubeh, without whom none of it would be possible. This essay traces ideas explored in the exhibition *Material Power: Palestinian Embroidery*, and I am extremely grateful to Andrew Nairne, Eliza Spindel and the team at Kettle's Yard, as well as to Amy George, Ann French, Victoria Hartley and the team at The Whitworth.

This publication emerged from an online lecture I was invited to give to Common Threads' global audience in March 2024. Many thanks to all those who signed up and watched the talk, as it was partly its popularity which prompted the brilliant Laura Moseley and Chris Shortt to suggest we turn it into a book. I can't thank Laura and Chris enough for their support, creative vision and care in this process, it's been a pleasure to work on it together. We're grateful to all the artists and organisations who granted us permission to use their images.

The original lecture was a fundraiser for Medical Aid for Palestinians, and proceeds from sales of this book will be donated to the Palestine Red Crescent Society to support its vital relief work in Gaza.

CREDITS

Installation view of *Material Power: Palestinian Embroidery* at Kettle's Yard, Cambridge.
Photos: Jo Underhill.

Material Power: Palestinian Embroidery installation at the Whitworth, The University of Manchester (2023).
Photos: Michael Pollard.

Arab Image Foundation
www.arabimagefoundation.org

Aya Haidar
www.ayahaidar.com

Hey Porter!
www.heyporterposter.com

Inaash Association
www.inaash.org

Maeve Brennan
www.maevebrennan.co.uk

The Palestinian Museum
www.palmuseum.org

The Palestine Poster Project Archives
www.palestineposterproject.org

Sliman Mansour
www.slimanmansour.com

Tiraz Centre
www.tirazcentre.org

Tirazain
www.tirazain.com

Amnesty International. "Israel/OPT: new restrictions on Palestinian flags an attempt to 'legitimise racism'." Press release. 11 January 2023.

Amnesty International. "Seventy+ Years of Suffocation." Accessed 8 June 2024. https://nakba.amnesty.org/en/about

Coates Urichsen, Kristian. *A Dictionary of Politics in the Middle East*. Oxford University Press, 2018.

Dedman, Rachel. *At the Seams: A Political History of Palestinian Embroidery*. The Palestinian Museum, 2016.

Dedman, Rachel, and Shuruq Harb, eds. *Labour of Love: New Approaches to Palestinian Embroidery*. The Palestinian Museum, 2018.

Ghnaim, Wafa. *Tatreez and Tea: Embroidery and Storytelling in the Palestinian Diaspora*. 2018.

Kawar, Widad. *Threads of Identity*. Rimal Books, 2011.

Nasir, Tania Tamari, Omar Joseph Nasser-Khoury, Shirabe Yamada, with Widad Kamel Kawar. *Seventeen Embroidery Techniques from Palestine: An Instruction Manual*. Sunbula, 2019.

Rejab, Jehan. *Palestinian Costume*. Kegan Paul International, 1989.

Sanchez Summerer, Karène, and Sary Zananiri, eds. *Imaging and Imagining Palestine: Photography, Modernity and the Biblical Lens, 1918–1948*. Brill, 2021.

Scholch, Alexander. "European penetration and the economic development of Palestine, 1856–82." In *Studies in the Economic and Social History of Palestine in the Nineteenth and Twentieth Centuries*, edited by Roger Owen. Southern Illinois University Press, 1982.

BIBLIOGRAPHY

Skinner, Margarita. *Palestinian Embroidery Motifs: A Treasury of Stitches, 1850–1950*. Rimal Books, 2007.

United Nations. "About the Nakba." Accessed 8 June 2024. https://www.un.org/unispal/about-the-nakba

Weir, Shelagh. *Embroidery from Palestine*. University of Washington Press, 2006.

Weir, Shelagh. *Palestinian Costume*. British Museum Press, London, 2004 (1989).

AUTHOR

Rachel Dedman (b. 1989, London) is a curator, writer, and art historian. Her work examines the material and political lives of things, and challenges established narratives around cultural production in the Global South. Since 2019, Rachel has been the Jameel Curator of Contemporary Art from the Middle East at the V&A, London, where she curates the triennial Jameel Prize exhibition and the Jameel Fellowship artist residency programme. Beyond the V&A, Rachel curated *Material Power: Palestinian Embroidery* for Kettle's Yard and The Whitworth, UK, in 2023/24, and was co-curator of the State of Fashion Biennale 2024: *Ties that Bind* in Arnhem, the Netherlands.

Between 2013 and 2019, Rachel was an independent curator based in Beirut, Lebanon. She curated exhibitions and projects across the Middle East and Europe, including for Beirut Art Centre, Ashkal Alwan, Sursock Museum (all Beirut), The Palestinian Museum (West Bank), apexart (New York), the Transart Triennale (Berlin), and Serpentine Galleries (London). Rachel holds a First-class degree in the history of art from St John's College, Oxford, where she was a Casberd Scholar, and was the Von Clemm Postgraduate Fellow at Harvard University, 2012/13. Her critical writing is widely published and she is the author of two books on Palestinian embroidery and dress. Rachel is currently Chair of the Board of Metroland Cultures, London.

www.racheldedman.com
@racheldedman

Common Threads Press is a small press dedicated to publishing books and zines about the radical histories of crafts and making.

Founded in 2019, our publications are written and developed in close collaboration with academics and artists alike, from all around the world, who share our deep love and critical interest in craft histories.

www.commonthreadspress.co.uk
@commonthreadspress

More from Common Threads Press:

**Diasporic Threads:
Black Women,
Fibre and Textiles**
Sharbreon Plummer
978-1-06862-505-3

**Softness:
A Meditation on Knitting**
Jean Oberlander
978-1-06862-504-6

**Many Hands Make a Quilt:
Short Histories of
Radical Quilting**
Jess Bailey
978-1-06862-502-2

**Mauka to Makai:
Hawaiian Quilts and the
Ecology of the Islands**
Marenka Thompson-Odlum
978-1-06862-500-8

**Stitching Freedom:
Embroidery & Incarceration**
Isabella Rosner
978-1-91632-347-6

**Rights Not Charity:
Protest Textiles and
Disability Activism**
Gill Crawshaw
978-1-91632-346-9

**The Norfolk Trans Joy
Community Quilt Zine**
Alice Bigsby-Bye,
Beau Brannick,
Poppy Marriott &
Laura Moseley
978-1-06862-503-9

**Slow Grown:
Plants, Folklore
& Natural Dyeing**
Ciara Callaghan
978-1-39992-032-2

**Stitching the Intifada:
Embroidery and Resistance
in Palestine**

ISBN: 978-1-06862-501-5

Written by Rachel Dedman
Edited by Laura Moseley
Designed by Chris Shortt

Typeset in AUTHENTIC Sans
(Christina Janus & Desmond
Wong) and Garibaldi (VocalType)

Cover motif (Shrba/Water) and
end marks (Qamar/Moon)
courtesy of Tirazain
www.tirazain.com

Front cover inside flap:
Intifada dress, 1987–1993,
from the collection of Tiraz:
Widad Kawar Home for Arab
Dress. Photo: Jo Underhill,
courtesy of Kettle's Yard,
Cambridge.

Back cover inside flap:
Sliman Mansour, *The Village
Awakens*, 1987. Courtesy of
the artist.

Printed and bound by Short Run
Press, Exeter, Devon, UK

Published 2024 by
Common Threads Press
www.commonthreadspress.co.uk

© Common Threads Press
and Rachel Dedman, 2024

All rights reserved. Contributions have been commissioned and therefore no part of this publication may be reproduced or copied in any form or by any means without permission of the copyright owners. Exceptions include the artists and authors sharing their own work, brief quotations, reviews and certain other non-commercial uses permitted by copyright law. The right of Rachel Dedman to be identified as author of this work has been asserted in accordance with Section 77 of the Copyright, Designs and Patents Act of 1988.

This publication was originally written to be delivered by the author at an online fundraising event by Common Threads Press on 25 March 2024.